A Writing Guide
for Business Professionals

A **Writing** Guide
for Business Professionals

◾ by Ellen Jovin

SYNTAXIS PRESS · NEW YORK

Published by Syntaxis Press®, a division of Syntaxis, Inc.
2109 Broadway, Suite 16-159
New York, New York 10023
www.syntaxis.com
info@syntaxis.com
(212) 799-3000

ISBN: 978-0-9785823-1-9
Library of Congress Control Number: 2006911326

Text set in Scala and Scala Sans
Design by Alton Creative, Inc.
Printed in the United States of America

9   8   7   6   5   4

Contents

Preface..vii

Introduction: Clarity in Business Writing.........................1

Chapter 1. Organization...5

1.1   Prewriting..7

1.2   Introductions..9

1.3   Order of Ideas..12

1.4   Development...15

1.5   Paragraph Length..17

1.6   Conclusions...18

1.7   Rewriting...19

Chapter 2. Sentence Structure.................................23

2.1   Sentence Structure Basics...................................24

2.2   Sentence Variety..26

2.3   Passive Voice...35

2.4   Excessive Use of Prepositional Phrases......................41

Chapter 3. Word Choice..45

3.1   Precision...45

3.2   Wordiness and Ornate Language...............................48

3.3   Jargon..50

3.4   Clichés...53

3.5   Excessive Use of Linking Verbs..............................54

**Chapter 4. E-Mail: Communication
in an Electronic Age**..59

4.1   Anatomy of an E-Mail Message................................60

      4.1.1   Salutations.............................62

4.1.2 Closings 67
4.1.3 Signature Files 69
4.2 Special Topics 71
4.2.1 Copying 71
4.2.2 Reply All 72
4.2.3 Forwarding 73
4.3 The Limitations of E-Mail 76

Chapter 5. Editing Your Writing: Tips and Tricks 79

Conclusion 91
Index 93

Preface

Words are the currency of virtually every business transaction. Words persuade. They educate. They clarify needs and intentions. Words inspire.

Nonetheless, many business professionals don't often stop to consider whether they are using words to their greatest advantage. The consequence: every day in every industry, organizational effectiveness is diminished by dull presentations, inappropriate or ungrammatical e-mail, and wordy, jargon-laden memos and reports. This book is one of a series of Syntaxis guides designed to combat problems such as these by developing oral and written communication skills needed in the workplace.

The advice offered in this series grew out of our experience training employees of leading firms in diverse industries. Based in New York City, Syntaxis conducts seminars in presentation skills, business writing, grammar, and e-mail etiquette throughout North America. The firm also provides one-on-one presentation skills coaching for senior executives.

These communication skills books are distributed to participants in Syntaxis training sessions, but they were designed to be standalone guides as well, for any professional who would like to speak and write more powerfully.

ELLEN JOVIN
Principal, Syntaxis

BRANDT JOHNSON
Principal, Syntaxis

Introduction

Clarity in
Business Writing

Good business writing requires clarity. Pressed for time, busy professionals simply do not want to sort through a document trying to figure out the writer's intentions. Unfortunately, many business documents are not as clear as they could — or should — be. The causes of this shortcoming are numerous, ranging from careless organization to unnecessarily complex syntax, to confusing rather than clarifying language.

The goal of this book is to help professionals develop a direct, natural communication style that supports rather than obscures what they want to say. The first three chapters focus on writing issues relevant for a wide range of business documents, including letters, memos, e-mail, reports, proposals, marketing materials, and more. A fourth chapter discusses writing issues unique to e-mail, the dominant form of written communication for many professionals today. The fifth chapter covers editing tips and tricks businesspeople can use to ensure that their documents are clear and polished.

Regardless of the document type, good business writing demands several things of a writer:

■ an understanding of audience

You must be aware of and sensitive to your intended audience's knowledge, needs, and motivations. For instance, if you are a lawyer writing for a lay audience, you should minimize legal jargon, define essential legal terms, and explain concepts so that a non-specialist can understand them. If you are writing a business plan for potential investors, you should show respect for your readers' time and informational needs by being concise and specific.

When you write something, you are generally trying to communicate ideas to someone who is different from you in myriad ways. The foundation of clear writing is the ability to put yourself in the position of the reader.

■ an understanding of subject matter

Good writing also depends on a solid grasp of the material; without it, a writer can't communicate clearly with other people. In a business environment, though, people must sometimes write about topics that are unfamiliar to them. If you find yourself in this situation, you should make every effort to educate yourself about your subject. Often one of the most time-consuming steps in the writing process is research.

■ good writing skills

Some people seem to be naturally gifted writers. Do not, however, make the mistake of assuming that either people have the ability to write or they don't. Many writing skills grow out of hard work and regular practice. Anyone can become a better writer.

■ careful rewriting

Most good writers are good at least in part because of the amount of effort they put into revising their work. They keep rewriting until they are satisfied with the results. Remember: the difference between good writing and bad writing is often rewriting.

Chapter 1
Organization

WELL-ORGANIZED WRITING conveys the maximum amount of information with the minimum amount of reader effort. Unfortunately, many writers (*writer* in this book refers to any professional who writes as part of his or her professional duties) pay insufficient attention to organizational issues, in part because figuring out how to improve a document's structure is time-consuming and even painful. It is, however, utterly necessary.

Theoretically, document organization in the computer age should be better than it was in the age of the typewriter. After all, in those pre-computer days, if you had been typing a seven-page document and realized while typing the fifth page that the last paragraph on that page should actually have been in the middle of your second page, would you have started over and retyped all those pages? Maybe, maybe not. (If you aren't old enough to recall the pre-computer days, you will need to use your imagination here.) The likelihood of your retyping would have depended on factors such as the importance of the document, your degree of motivation, the proximity of your deadline, and your typing speed.

In the computer age, however, if you realize that a paragraph on page 5 should be on page 2, it will take you only a few seconds to move it (plus, of course, the amount of time needed to smooth out the word choice in both locations so that everything flows properly).

Theory and practice do not always coincide, unfortunately, and in fact, the quality of document organization seems to have declined rather dramatically over the past generation. The problem may be in part that people *know* they can move things around easily. Consequently, instead of thinking through structure and content before they begin to type — as they would have done in the typewriter days — many businesspeople have a writing process something like this: Turn on the computer, start typing, keep typing until several pages have been completed, go to lunch with the intention of revising afterwards, return to one's desk, read over the document, decide it's not so bad after all, add a hard return in the middle of an extra-long paragraph, add a few transitional expressions to make the ideas flow better (an *in addition* here, a *however* there, a *moreover* somewhere else), run the grammar-checker and spell-checker, attach the document to an e-mail, and press "Send."

Now, transitional expressions are wonderful

things, but they are wholly inadequate as cures for bad organization. Adding a *furthermore* to the beginning of a sentence to try to make it *sound* as though it is related to the previous sentence, even when it really isn't, is like putting a small adhesive bandage on a gaping wound. That simply won't suffice; the wound must first be treated.

To fix organizational weaknesses, the writer must look very carefully at content, independent of word choice, and consider whether the way a given piece of writing is structured really makes sense. This chapter covers an array of organizational issues applicable to diverse business documents.

1.1 **Prewriting**

Careful writing generally involves a three-part process that consists first of prewriting, then the actual writing of a draft, and finally, rewriting. Most people focus too much on the writing stage, at the expense of the prewriting and rewriting stages.

Prewriting is important because it helps ensure that you consider a full spectrum of ideas *before* you start your first draft. It can consist of various activities, including:

■ Research and note-taking

In order to know what you want to say, you must first be familiar with your subject. If your writing project requires research, read about your topic online, in other documents your organization has published previously, in magazines, or anywhere else you can find relevant, reliable information. You may want to interview colleagues or, in some cases, clients to help you gather necessary information. You will probably want to take notes throughout the research process.

■ Brainstorming

Take out a piece of paper (or open a new file on your computer) and list any and all thoughts you have on your topic. Phrases and sentence fragments are fine, even preferable; at this stage you should not concern yourself with grammar. Also, do not worry about whether your ideas are good or bad. Turn off that critical voice in your head, and simply write down everything that occurs to you, from details to general ideas to possible counterarguments.

■ Freewriting

Freewriting exercises are particularly helpful for people who suffer from writer's block. As with brainstorming, take out a blank piece of paper — or, if you are electronically inclined, open a new file — and just start writing about your topic. The only rule of freewriting is: do not stop writing! Unlike brainstorming, freewriting involves writing in more or less standard sentences and, if you like, paragraphs. If you run out of ideas, simply write something like *I can't think of anything I need some coffee my left foot hurts* and so on until something occurs to you. Do not worry about grammar, spelling, or the quality of your ideas.

In prewriting, you unlock your creativity. Maybe some of the things you write down won't be relevant. That's fine. But at least you will have some words to work with—a crucial first step!

Once you have completed any necessary research, brainstormed, and/or tried a freewriting exercise, examine what you have so far and start to consider what you might include in your document and how it could be arranged. Some people like to create an outline, which is an extremely valuable thing to do before writing a draft.

Suppose you're not quite ready to outline, though. In that case, you can instead read through the research you've collected, or perhaps look at a list of ideas you created through brainstorming. If you take that list and start crossing off irrelevant ideas, marking ideas that you would like to use, drawing arrows to connect related points, and so on, you may begin to get a sense of possible structure for your memo, report, or whatever document you happen to be writing.

1.2 **Introductions**

The requirements of an introduction are fairly

consistent across various types of business documents. The introduction should help the reader understand what will be covered in the **body** of a document (i.e., everything between the introduction and the conclusion) and should contain your **thesis**, or main idea. If you can't express that main idea in a sentence or two, you should keep thinking, writing, and rewriting until you can. This holds true whether you are composing a business letter, a proposal, or any other type of document.

Many people are diligent about trying to convey their main point, but then neglect a critical second purpose of an introduction: to engage the reader. Upon finishing your introduction, your reader should want to continue reading! Now, engaging readers is not an easy task, and your success at it depends on a number of factors: clear, dynamic word choice; streamlined, readable sentences; a logical flow of ideas; and careful consideration of what your reader already knows or wants to know. These issues will be addressed in more detail as you continue through this book.

How long is a good introduction? There is no official minimum or maximum, though the typical introduction consists of no more than a paragraph. In some cases — for example, in complex reports — the introduction may extend to a few paragraphs, but the vast majority of openings can be confined to a single paragraph consisting of roughly two to five sentences. The precise length depends in part on the projected length of the entire document and on the nature and complexity of the content you need to introduce.

Some people write their introduction last, after they have completed a draft of their document. Other people find it more productive to write a working introduction first. Then, once they have finished a full draft, they return to the introduction and revise it. Regardless of your approach, you will probably find it necessary to revise your introduction multiple times before it describes the point of your document in a concise, clear, and interesting way.

Below are some of the most common weaknesses afflicting introductions. Look for them as you revise.

■ The introduction is too broad.

If an introduction is too general, it won't be useful to the reader. Make sure your introduction is specific enough (though not excessively so) that your reader will understand what you are trying to say. Your opening shouldn't be broader in its scope than the content covered in the body.

■ The introduction is too narrow.

The introduction should act as a kind of thematic umbrella for the body of your document. If the body includes ideas that do not truly fit under this thematic umbrella, then you will need to keep rewriting until there is a match. That doesn't mean your introduction has to list every topic you will be discussing; it just means that those topics should fit inside the larger theme or themes you present in that opening.

■ **The introduction consists primarily or entirely of details.**

For example, if you were writing a memo about why your company needed to change stationery vendors, your introduction could not consist solely of an anecdote regarding a recent problem you had with a paper-clip order. That example could perhaps serve as an interesting hook to begin your introduction, but you would still need to include a thesis that clarified your document's larger purpose.

1.3 Order of Ideas

The order of ideas in a piece of business writing varies based on content and goals. However, your ideas should unfold in a way that is as easy as possible for the reader to understand.

For the body of your document — again, everything except your introduction and conclusion — it can be helpful to keep in mind these general organizational principles:

1. In many business documents, the most important ideas should appear first, with less im-

portant ideas appearing later.

Why? Your readers will be more likely to continue reading if the ideas seem significant. In addition, if a reader is unavoidably interrupted, at least he or she will have read your most important points.

2. In other documents, ideas form a logical chain.

With this structure, each point follows logically from the previous idea and leads logically to the next. In a technical report for a business audience, for example, you may be explaining complex ideas to people who are unfamiliar with your subject matter. To succeed, you must think like a teacher, introducing ideas one at a time to your audience and explaining each one clearly before you move on to the next. You may actually end up developing your most important idea last — after you have explained all the preceding concepts the reader must be familiar with in order to understand your big idea.

Training materials and user guides are examples of document types that frequently rely on this organizational scheme.

3. Content is often presented in chronological order.

Many business documents contain narratives, details, or examples that are best explained in chronological order. In other words, the writer starts at the beginning, proceeds to the middle, and concludes with the end. An anecdote or example can last a couple of sentences or multiple pages. Unfortunately, some businesspeople overuse chronological structures in cases where another organizational principle — principle 1 above, for example — might be better.

For instance, consider these organizational principles in the context of a specific document type: the executive biography. Suppose you went to a company's website and found the biography for the firm's chief financial officer. How would you expect that to be structured? Most important idea(s) first? Logical order? Chronological order?

Although some executive bios are structured chronologically — in other words, starting with where the person was born and then proceeding to educational background, first professional position, second professional position, and so on, until the writer reaches the current position — that is a fairly unusual approach. Most bios begin with the executive's current role and then proceed backwards in time. Why? Because the current position is — unless the person is on a downward professional spiral! — generally the most senior, responsible, important position he or she has held. It is certainly the most important for the company on whose website the bio appears. Thus, the typical executive bio actually fits the first organizational scheme: most significant idea first.

Keep in mind that, especially with long documents, the choice of organizational structure is not necessarily an all-or-nothing decision. Principle 1 may be at work in one section of a document, while 2 and 3 may dominate in other segments.

1.4 **Development**

You must explain your ideas adequately in the body of your document; in other words, you must *develop* them. The reader should not have to labor to understand what you mean; rather, you—the writer—should do the work for the reader.

Thus, complex points must be allotted time and space sufficient for the reader to understand them. General statements should be supported with details and examples.

At first glance, the paragraph below may seem to contain the supporting details needed to explain its main idea, which appears in the first sentence.

> The grocery store manager received a negative performance review. According to his supervisor, he had poor people skills, a bad temper, and a negative attitude.

What, however, are poor people skills? And how did the manager's bad temper and negative attitude manifest themselves?

Now compare the paragraph below with the preceding example.

> The grocery store manager received a negative performance review. According to his supervisor, when colleagues disagreed with him, he repeatedly showed an inability to compromise. In addition, he frequently exploded in rage over trivial incidents — for example, screaming at a clerk who accidentally knocked over some cans he had just stacked near the register. Finally, he regularly belittled the store's prospects, maintaining that the supermarket on the next block would make it impossible for the store to succeed in that area.

The revised version contains concrete details and creates a more complete picture of the problem. The first paragraph did not develop its main idea; the second does.

Now, imagine you are an editor of a college newspaper, reviewing an article someone has submitted for possible publication. The article tells job applicants how to improve their job prospects. One of the body paragraphs reads as follows:

> By dressing appropriately, job applicants increase their chances of finding work. In addition, a carefully edited résumé conveys professionalism.

By the second sentence of this two-sentence

paragraph, the writer has prematurely abandoned the question of appropriate interview attire for a new topic: the résumé. Since the article was written for a college paper, we can assume that the audience consists of inexperienced job seekers. Therefore, the writer needs to explain very specifically what appropriate attire entails, from ties and suits to shoes and jewelry.

Only when the writer has clarified some of these sartorial details can he or she then move on to the question of résumé editing.

1.5 **Paragraph Length**

Imagine you are reading a report on your business unit's performance during the third quarter. Nearly every paragraph takes up about half of a single-spaced, typed page — page after page after page. What is the effect on you, the reader?

Probably exhaustion, because the writer has most likely included too many ideas in each paragraph, thus leaving it up to you to understand which sentences go together and what the relationship among the various ideas is.

Generally, a body paragraph should contain one main idea, often called the **topic sentence**, on which the writer elaborates. There are exceptions, but many paragraphs follow this format — and many of those that don't, should.

When you signal the start of a new paragraph (by indenting, or skipping a line, or both), you are signaling to the reader the start of a new thought. Paragraphing is an example of how form—in other words, the appearance of a document—supports content.

Now, imagine you are reading a report that strings together a series of extremely short paragraphs. Is this an improvement over the collection of excessively long paragraphs? Not necessarily. Writers who overuse short paragraphs often create a choppy, disjointed effect.

As in most things, moderation—manifested through a mixture of short, medium-length, and longer paragraphs—is often the best approach.

1.6 Conclusions

Most business documents need a conclusion that reminds the reader of the writer's key points. Usually a good conclusion will be a paragraph in length, though just as with the introduction, a longer, more complex document may require a somewhat longer conclusion.

In creating a conclusion, one of the biggest challenges writers face is how to close a document without simply repeating, in the same or similar words, what has already appeared in the introduction or elsewhere in the document. Remember, though, when your readers reach the conclusion, they will have traveled quite a distance (even if only a page) since the introduction. You, the writer, will presumably have explained your ideas, provided examples and details, and left your readers more educated about your topic than they were at the beginning. Because of your readers' greater understanding, you can go a step further in your conclusion than you did in your introduction.

For example, in the conclusion of a report you might tie together your main ideas while commenting on their implication for the future. In a memo, you might summarize issues discussed in the body of the document while also emphasizing for the readers what action you would like them to take.

If you are stuck, take a step back and think about the larger practical and philosophical importance of what you have written. Why does it matter? What do you want your reader to do or think about your topic? Your conclusion is an opportunity to bring home the piece's significance in a way that is difficult to do at the beginning, when you are introducing brand new ideas.

1.7 **Rewriting**

You have completed a draft of your business letter, memo, or whatever it is you happen to be writing. You feel a tremendous sense of relief. It is not, however, time to pull out the party hats!

A careful writer knows that finishing a draft is only one stage of the writing process. Rewriting is where the action is. Go through your document paragraph by paragraph, thinking critically about each one and how it relates to the paragraphs before and after it. Eliminate needless repitition.

You should then go through the same process on the sentence level as well, checking the relationship of each sentence to the other sentences around it in a paragraph and again deleting unnecessary repitition of ideas.

Finally, every paragraph and every sentence should relate back to your document's main idea. Chapter 5 includes a series of editing checklists that can help you with this process.

Chapter 2
Sentence Structure

GOOD SENTENCE STRUCTURE is essential to good writing; it adds both clarity and interest. Poor sentence structure can befuddle or weary the audience, making the task of reading more unpleasant than informative.

One important way to enliven a piece of writing is to vary the length and structure of your sentences. Try reading aloud something you have written. Listen to the rhythm and flow of the sentences. Is there interest and variety? Or do you feel as though there is a kind of repetitive drone? If the latter is the case, you may be in a sentence structure rut! Try mixing things up a bit. Vary sentence length. Vary the way you combine ideas.

Some writers overuse long, convoluted sentences, obscuring their ideas behind complex syntax. Busy professionals simply do not want to re-read sentences to try to figure out what the writer meant. On the other hand, if a piece of writing contains too many short, simple sentences in a row, the writing may sound choppy and unsophisticated, and the reader could lose interest.

A simple, punchy idea might be best expressed with a simple sentence structure. A more complicated idea may justify a longer, more complex sentence structure. A mixture of sentence types can make the act of reading your writing a more pleasurable and productive experience for your audience.

2.1 **Sentence Structure Basics**

To understand sentence structure, you must first be able to identify a **clause**: a group of grammatically related words that includes a subject and a predicate.

A **subject** is a noun or pronoun that performs the action in a clause or that the clause is about.

The **physician** called the lab.

The **restaurant** had no tables available.

The **CFO** will announce first-quarter results today.

A **predicate** consists of one or more verbs and accompanying modifiers.

Subject · *Predicate*

The **attorney** *worked all night on her speech.*

Greg's previous **manager** *accepted a position at a competing firm.*

Sue and **John** *have submitted an impressive proposal.*

The third example above contains a compound subject consisting of two proper nouns (in other words, names). In addition, all three of the preceding examples are **independent clauses**. That means they are clauses that can stand alone as sentences.

A second clause type is called **dependent**, meaning it cannot stand alone. A dependent clause — also known as a **subordinate clause** — begins with a **subordinating conjunction**. There are dozens of subordinating conjunctions; the partial list below offers a representative sampling.

after	since
although	so that
as	unless
as if	until
because	when
before	whenever
even though	whereas
if	while

In each of the following dependent clauses, the subordinating conjunction launches the clause, which also includes a subject and predicate.

<u>Subordinating Conjunction</u> • **Subject** • *Predicate*

<u>because</u> **he** *forgot his umbrella*

when **Ms. Richards** *called me*

until the **president** *arrives*

To turn the dependent clauses above into independent clauses, simply remove the subordinating conjunction:

He *forgot his umbrella.*

Ms. Richards *called me.*

The **president** *arrives.*

2.2 **Sentence Variety**

This section covers some common sentence types and considers the stylistic consequences of overusing certain structures — or of avoiding them altogether.

Consider the following group of words:

Revenues were plummeting we decided to close two branches.

That group of words contains two clauses — both independent — with no punctuation or combining word to link them. This is a classic example of a **run-on sentence**: two independent clauses joined together with nothing but air.

The way you link ideas such as those contained in the run-on above has everything to do with sentence style and readability. Below are the main options for punctuating and/or combining these ideas, with commentary on the stylistic nuances of each.

Version 1. **Period**

> Revenues were plummeting. We decided to close two branches.

Although using occasional very short sentences can be a powerful writing technique, these two short sentences sound choppy next to each other.

Version 2. **Semicolon**

> Revenues were plummeting; we decided to close two branches.

Here the two independent clauses are combined with a semicolon. How does this version differ from Version 1? Well, punctuation marks are often described as the traffic signals of writing. You could associate the comma with a rolling stop at a stop sign, a semicolon with a quick (but fully legal!) stop at the same sign, and a period with a brief wait at a red light.

Linked with a semicolon, these two clauses read more quickly than they did when separated by a period. Some people, unfortunately, are semicolonphobic; they never use semicolons, largely because they don't know how. While there is no minimum daily requirement for the semicolon, any time you eliminate one entire sentence-combining method because you are uncomfortable with it, you are by definition limiting the range of stylistic options available to you.

THE DREADED COMMA SPLICE

 Many businesspeople today are in the habit of combining two independent clauses with just a comma, like this:

Revenues were plummeting, we decided to close two branches.

Unfortunately, the sentence above is actually a sentence error called a *comma splice*. If you are writing a creative piece—a poem or novel, for example—you may occasionally find stylistic reasons to use a comma splice. Business writing, however, is a place for traditional punctuation, not experimentation. Think of the comma as being too frail, too delicate a piece of punctuation to hold apart two independent clauses without the additional help of some kind of combining word.

Remember: in business writing, where you can put a period you can virtually never put a comma. If you do, you will in most cases create a comma splice. Periods and commas are like punctuation enemies; though they may be distant relatives, they do not get along and do not hang out in the same kinds of places.

Below are the criteria that justify semicolon use between two independent clauses:

1. The ideas being linked are closely related.

2. When you read the sentence aloud, it sounds good; the ideas flow.

Version 2 (on page 27) may not be an award-winning sentence, but it sounds reasonably good. Whether it works in a given document would depend in part on the surrounding sentences and how they are structured.

Version 3. **Coordinating Conjunction**

Revenues were plummeting, so we decided to close two branches.

Coordinating conjunctions such as *so* combine sentence elements of roughly equal weight. There are seven such conjunctions in all. To remember them, think **fanboys**; it isn't a word, but it sounds like one. Each letter in fanboys represents the first letter of one of the seven coordinating conjunctions:

for   or
and   yet
nor   so
but

Many businesspeople rely too heavily on coordinating conjunctions as a way of linking ideas. Coordinating conjunctions are useful—in fact, critically important—words in the English language, but overusing them creates writing problems. Because they link elements of similar weight, when they are overused as clause-combining tools, a piece of writing can start to feel like an accumulation of ideas and details, without a sense of hierarchy or a sufficiently sturdy structure. This and that. This so that. This but that. This or that. To add variety to your writing style, be sure to use other idea-combining options, too.

In Version 3 on the preceding page, note the comma before the *so*. If you use a coordinating conjunction to combine two independent clauses, it is standard punctuation to include a comma before the conjunction. One exception could be two very short clauses combined with an *and*. In many other cases, leaving the comma out can confuse readers or at least make it more difficult for them to identify the boundary between two ideas.

Version 4. **Conjunctive Adverb**

Revenues were plummeting; therefore, we decided to close two branches.

Therefore is an example of a conjunctive adverb—in other words, a conjunction-like adverb. There are many such adverbs, though the following five show up particularly often in business writing:

    therefore
    furthermore
    however
    moreover
    nevertheless

The structure of Version 4 on the preceding page is in some ways similar to Version 3, but there are stylistic differences that a writer should be aware of, particularly if he or she is, ahem, a conjunctive adverb addict. Conjunctive adverb addiction is particularly common among consultants, attorneys, and academics, but it can be found in virtually every industry.

The overuse of conjunctive adverbs creates a rather ponderous, heavy writing style. Why? First of all, many conjunctive adverbs are on the formal end of the style spectrum. Also, if you look at Version 4, you will see that there are two breaks in the middle of the sentence: a significant break associated with the semicolon, followed by a fairly formal polysyllabic word (the conjunctive adverb), and then another break associated with the comma.

In isolation, there's nothing wrong with a structure like that. Imagine, though, a document in which the writer repeatedly uses this structure to combine clauses. It's a slower structure, with more stops and starts, and more attention drawn to the intersection between ideas, than you see in Version 3. Once again, as with most things, moderation is the key.

Version 5. **Subordinating Conjunction**

5a. Because revenues were plummeting, we decided to close two branches.

5b. We decided to close two branches because revenues were plummeting.

Versions 5a and 5b illustrate the use of the subordinating conjunction *because* to combine ideas. In 5a, the subordinating conjunction appears at the beginning, thus turning that first clause into a dependent clause, which is then followed by an independent clause (*we decided to close two branches*). In 5b, the sentence begins with an independent clause that is then followed by a dependent clause.

Either sentence is fine, but when asked which they prefer, many people will automatically choose 5b. When asked *why* they prefer it, the response is often: "I was told in school never to begin a sentence with *because*." But this ostensible rule is nothing more than a writing myth.

In fact, the prejudice against *because* as a sentence starter leads to numerous writing problems, as professionals go through all sorts of language contortions to avoid what is a perfectly good sentence structure. In avoiding it unnecessarily, they impoverish their writing style, because Version 5a has a dramatic structure and offers an interesting alternative to the plain subject-verb format.

Consider that same structure applied to even more dramatic content:

> Because he embezzled millions of dollars, he spent the rest of his life in jail.

Unfortunately, many people will automatically flip these two clauses to eliminate the starting *because*:

> He spent the rest of his life in jail because he embezzled millions of dollars.

But flipping the clauses sucks much of the life and energy from the sentence.

Other people will meticulously cross out *because* and replace it with *due to the fact that*.

> Due to the fact that he embezzled millions of dollars, he spent the rest of his life in jail.

This structure is wordy, awkward, and inherently inferior to the version beginning with *because*.

For those who remain uncomfortable with the idea of beginning with *because*: if you have spent your whole life avoiding *because* at the beginnings of sentences, but have at the same time been starting sentences with *if,* or *when,* or *while,* you may have inadvertently been guilty of grammatical hypocrisy! The following four sentences are structurally identical; each starts with a dependent clause and concludes with an independent clause:

> Because her train was delayed, Sue missed the meeting.
>
> If her train is delayed, Sue will catch a cab.

THE *Because* MYTH

 Why do so many teachers tell students not to begin sentences with *because*? After all, this writing "rule" was—and is—bad advice, ignored by good writers everywhere.

Presumably, some teachers believe this prohibition to be legitimate, but others may view it as a practical means to an end, without necessarily believing it to be a requirement for good grammar. Consider, after all, the favorite question of every small child: "Why?" The answer, inevitably, begins with *because.* Left to their own devices, many children will write things like the following:

I like going to the beach. Because there are waves.

The problem with the second piece—*because there are waves*—is not that it begins with *because*, but that it is a fragment, a mere piece of a sentence. But if grade school

When her train is delayed, Sue catches a cab.

While Sue was waiting for her train, she called one of her colleagues.

There is nothing wrong with any of them.

2.3   **Passive Voice**

Perhaps you have been told before not to use passive voice, examples of which abound in business writing. The idea, though, is not to eliminate pas-

or junior high school teachers tried to offer their students a grammatical explanation of when they could begin with *because* and when they couldn't, it might sound something like this: "You may begin with *because* if your dependent clause is followed by an independent clause, but if your sentence consists of a single clause, you may not begin with *because*."

Phew! After a generation of inadequate grammar instruction in many American schools, blank stares, not illumination, would be the likely result of this explanation. Some teachers may find it easier to issue a blanket edict against beginning with *because*, hoping that somewhere in their students' educational futures, another teacher will clarify the issue in more detail.

Unfortunately, for many people that moment never arrives. The result is that this misconception continues to keep writers from expressing their ideas as directly and powerfully as they might.

sive voice entirely; rather, you should avoid excessive or unjustified use of passive voice.

To reduce passive voice, one must first be able to identify it. The sentence below offers a classic example:

The results were analyzed by the executive committee.

What makes this sentence passive? Look for the following characteristics:

1. The grammatical subject — *results,* in this example — receives the action of the verb. In other words, the results don't do anything; rather, something is done to them.

2. The verbs include the following:

a. a form of the verb *to be* (*were,* in this case). Besides *were,* other forms of *to be* are as follows: *am, is, are, was, be, been,* and *being.*

b. a **past participle** (here, the word *analyzed*)

In case the past participle is a hazy memory (or no memory at all!), just keep in mind that it is the form of a verb that would fit in the following blank: *I have* _____. For regular verbs, the past participle is identical to the past tense (*I have moved* vs. *I moved*, *I have finished* vs. *I finished*, etc.). For irregular verbs, the past participle and past tense differ. For instance, the past participle of *to drive* is *driven*, while the past tense is *drove*. The past participle of *to eat* is *eaten*, while the past tense is *ate*.

3. If the entity performing the action is included in the sentence, it typically follows the verbs and appears as part of a **prepositional phrase** — in the example above, *by the executive committee*. (For more on prepositional phrases, see Section 2.4.) A sentence can contain passive voice without including this information, though. Deleting *by the executive committee* from the sample sentence does not eliminate the passive voice. The following is still a passive construction:

> The results were analyzed.

As you look for passive voice, keep in mind that a form of the verb *to be* does not automatically signal a passive construction. For example, how many of the following three sentences contain passive voice?

1. The meeting was not productive for me.

2. The meeting was led by Edna.

3. The meeting was boring the attendees.

In fact, only the second sentence illustrates passive voice. In Sentence 1, *productive* is an adjective, not a past participle. In the third sentence, *boring* is not a past participle either. (Remember, it can't fit in the following blank: *I have _____.*) In addition, the subject of the sentence — *meeting* — is performing the action, namely, boring the attendees. Sentence 3 is actually a perfect example of **active voice**.

■ REDUCING PASSIVE VOICE

In many passive-voice constructions, the writer would be better off rewriting the sentence using active voice. Compare these two versions:

Passive Voice

The results were analyzed by the executive committee.

Active Voice

The executive committee analyzed the results.

Active voice is generally superior to passive voice. For one thing, it is more direct. The reader learns first who or what performed the action, then what the action was, and finally who or what was acted upon. It is usually easier to process information that way than it is to begin with the recipient of the action, then learn what the action was, then find out who did it.

Also, by replacing passive with active voice in the example above, we reduced the number of words by two. Active voice is in most cases the more economical structure.

Watch out for passive-voice constructions such as the following, which recur frequently in business documents:

- it is recommended that
- it was decided that
- it has been noted that

In many cases, these phrases are fillers and can simply be eliminated, often with little or no rewriting of the remainder of the sentences that contain them. Compare the original and revised versions of the following sentences (passive voice is italicized):

Original

It was decided that we need to shut down our Oregon plant.

Improved

Unfortunately, we need to shut down our Oregon plant.

Original

It has been noted that employees have been using their corporate e-mail accounts to send personal messages.

Improved

Employees have been using their corporate e-mail accounts to send personal messages.

■ ACCEPTABLE PASSIVE VOICE

Nonetheless, passive voice is sometimes acceptable, even preferable. For example, it is appropriate in the following cases:

1. when the entity performing the action is unknown

Suppose your cat comes home one night with a cut on her leg, and you don't know the cause of the injury. When you go into work the next day, you might tell your assistant, "My cat was injured last night." If you don't know how your cat was injured, it is hard to construct a reasonable active-voice version of this sentence. You might have to say something silly like, "A dog, another cat, or maybe something else altogether injured my cat last night."

2. when the emphasis is properly on the entity receiving the action

For example, you might complain to the head of the marketing department, "Our website hasn't been updated in nearly six months." Here, passive voice emphasizes the fact that your website isn't current. Now, if you wanted to assign blame for this problem, you would probably gravitate towards active voice instead: "You haven't updated our website in nearly six months."

2.4 **Excessive Use of Prepositional Phrases**

A prepositional phrase consists of two parts: (1) a preposition and (2) the object of the preposition, which is a noun or pronoun, accompanied by any modifiers. Following are some examples of prepositional phrases:

Preposition · *Object*

in the conference *room*
under the *rug*
near the birch *tree*
over my *head*
during John's *meeting*
before your *call*

Some writers have a tendency to overuse prepositional phrases, repeatedly stringing together four, five, or even more in a row. They are often motivated by the desire to convey a lot of information quickly, but the result can be a meandering sentence structure that is difficult to follow. Try reading the following sentence aloud (prepositional phrases are indicated with parentheses):

The first half (of the new book) (by Roberta Durang) (about the early history) (of XYZ Corporation), one (of the first high-tech companies) (in Arkansas), includes some remarkable stories (of industry-transforming technological innovation).

Now read aloud this revised version, which breaks the original sentence into two:

> XYZ Corporation was one (of the first high-tech companies) (in Arkansas). (In her new book) (on the company's early history), writer Roberta Durang tells some remarkable stories (of industry-transforming technological innovation).

The new version is much easier to follow. Dividing the original sentence improves readability, as does reducing the number of consecutive prepositional phrases. Whereas the first example contains an awkward cluster of six prepositional phrases, the second has eliminated this awkwardness. In addition, even though the revised example contains two sentences, it is shorter by two words than the original one-sentence version.

Increasing the number of sentences can sometimes actually help you reduce the overall number of words!

Chapter 3
Word Choice

To WRITE POWERFULLY, you must carefully select the words you use, considering whether in any given case there is another word that could express an idea more clearly. Good word choice is essential for lively, engaging writing.

3.1 **Precision**

Much business writing suffers from a lack of precision, largely because it is more difficult to be specific than it is to be vague. Specific writing requires more careful thought and more thoughtful writing and rewriting.

Suppose you are a managing director reading an annual performance review that one of your vice presidents wrote about an employee, Brad, in your department. You encounter the following sentence, which appears in the review without elaboration:

Brad does consistently sloppy work.

You have no way of knowing what exactly is meant by *sloppy*. Does he have messy handwriting?

Does he spill his lunch on his documents? Does he fail to proofread his e-mail carefully?

Let's replace the above sentence with the following:

Brad's proposals consistently contain mathematical and other factual errors.

Now we—and Brad's managing director, and Brad himself—can understand what the problem is. Perhaps Brad will have a chance to improve the quality of his proposals, enhance his overall performance, and ultimately contribute more to the company. This example illustrates how good writing can be good business.

It can be useful to think of your blank screen, or blank piece of paper, as an artist's blank canvas. Unless you paint your ideas clearly on that page, your audience won't see what you wish to communicate. Where relevant, it helps if you use language that appeals to one or more of the five senses: sight, smell, sound, taste, and touch.

For instance, imagine you must write a brochure promoting a new hotel. Compare these two sentences:

All of our rooms overlook a beautiful lake.

From your room, you can look out over the blue waters of Charles Pond, home to dozens of turtles and a pair of swans.

What is the difference between the two? Unlike the first sentence, the second appeals to the senses with specific visual images. You can actually picture the scene.

Which of the two sentences is more tempting marketing copy? Unless you have a strong aversion to turtles and swans, you will probably respond more positively to the second.

Besides specificity, precise writing requires the right word for the right occasion. Consider the following sentence:

> During the next year, we intend to accelerate our market share in the financial services sector.

The writer has misused the word *accelerate*, which involves increasing the speed of something. Since one can't increase the speed of market share, this is the wrong word. In this case, the more mundane — and more accurate — *increase* would be a good substitute.

Editing for word choice problems requires a critical eye and attention to detail. It also requires a good dictionary. Early drafts will naturally contain wording problems.

As with other rewriting activities, you may get better results if you can put a document away for a while and return to it fresh at a later time.

3.2 **Wordiness and Ornate Language**

Writers sometimes use a hundred words where fifty would do. This tendency, known as wordiness, weakens writing in several ways.

First, it shows a lack of respect for the reader's time and suggests that the writer has not bothered to revise sufficiently. In business, wasted time means wasted money.

Second, verbosity obscures the writer's ideas by hiding them amid a word surplus. Is it easier to find a needle in a haystack or to find a needle amid a few wisps of straw?

Finally, wordiness frequently signals to the reader that the writer is seeking to hide a lack of substance.

Related to wordiness is the tendency to use unnaturally ornate expressions in an effort to dress up a piece of writing. Why write *is cognizant of* when you can substitute *is aware of* or *knows about*? Why write *due to the fact that* when *because* will do? The answer is: there is no reason. Straightforward, succinct language will draw less attention to itself and keep the reader's attention on your message.

Business correspondence frequently contains unnecessarily ornate expressions such as *please find attached* or *pursuant to your request*. Just as these expressions would sound stilted in speech, they sound stilted in e-mails, letters, and memos. Replace them with more direct, natural language, as illustrated in the table below.

Ornate Expression	More Natural Alternative
please find attached attached please find	I have attached *or* attached is
please find enclosed enclosed please find	I have enclosed *or* enclosed is
please be advised that	[nothing] *or* please note that
per your request as per your request pursuant to your request	as you requested
per our conversation as per our conversation	as we discussed

Eliminating problematic phrases can dramatically improve your writing style. Consider the effect of a few simple word-choice substitutions in the following pairs of sentences.

Unnecessarily Ornate	Revised
Pursuant to your request, please find attached the status report.	As you requested, I have attached the status report.

Unnecessarily Ornate	**Revised**
Please be advised that the conference will end at 4:00 instead of 3:30.	The conference will end at 4:00 instead of 3:30.
As per our conversation, I have asked Deirdre to research the new location.	As we discussed, I have asked Deirdre to research the new location.

3.3 Jargon

Various professions have their own specialized vocabulary, called *jargon*. Lawyers, computer programmers, physicians, and many other professionals regularly use words that are familiar to their colleagues but mysterious to people in other disciplines.

If you are a biochemist writing for other biochemists, it would be natural and appropriate to refer to *organelles, bioassays,* or even *colloidal inorganic semiconductor nanocrystals.* However, a specialist who is writing for a lay audience has an obligation to explain any terms that might be unfamiliar to readers. A bond-fund manager will know what mortgage-backed securities are, but if she is writing an article for an audience of inexperienced investors, she should explain the term before using it.

In addition to profession-specific jargon, the business community in general is constantly developing its own vocabulary. Some of these new words are useful and fill a need, but many of them are trendy and vague and contribute little to clarity. Examples of questionable business terminology include:

actionable
best of breed
best practices
core competencies
enterprise-wide
incent/incentivize/disincent
mission-critical
operationalize
optimize
proactive
synergy/synergies/synergize
value-added, value add

Most of the terms included on this list are so widely used that you may be surprised to see them here. (And if you don't recognize them, that may be a good sign!)

Imagine you are reading a memo on business strategy in which the writer uses these terms prolifically. In the memo you encounter the following sentence: "We need to proactively operationalize our core competencies enterprise-wide to ensure synergies and value adds for all of our clients."

Would you understand what that meant? Would the writer himself understand what that meant? Probably not. Now, this example is perhaps a little exaggerated, but not by much; this type of fluffy writing is all too common in business.

If you regularly use terms such as *operationalize* or *synergize* in your own writing, try the following experiment. Write down a definition of the terms, and then ask a colleague to define the same terms. Now compare your definitions.

Chances are good that (1) one or both of you will have had a hard time defining the terms, which suggests their meaning is elusive, and/or (2) your definitions won't be the same, even if you haven't had trouble composing them.

Remember: communication depends on consensus about the meanings of words. If people cannot generally agree on a word's definition, they will not be able to communicate effectively when they use it.

A final type of jargon is the **acronym**, formed by combining the initial letters of a series of words—for example, *ATO* for *Approved Training Office*. Acronyms are popular in business writing because they save space (and perhaps, in some cases, because they sound technical and intimidating). Acronyms are often a convenience to the writer rather than to the reader, though, and when overused, can confuse and frustrate your audience. Writing etiquette requires that you put the reader's comfort and convenience before any desire you may have to reduce keystrokes.

Of course, if your readers are already reasonably familiar with an acronym you wish to use, or if the acronym is intuitive and easy to learn, then you can do the following:

1. Write out the first reference in full, followed by the acronym in parentheses, as in this example:

> The second chapter discusses collateralized
> loan obligations (CLOs).

2. For subsequent references, use only the acronym.

3.4 **Clichés**

Clichés are trite expressions. They have been worn out through overuse and should thus be avoided. Examples include:

> off the radar screen
> on the radar screen
> on a going-forward basis
> think outside the box
> stay ahead of the curve
> drop the ball

Clichés act as a kind of verbal sedative: they dramatically reduce the likelihood that the reader will heed your message. If you want your reader to pay attention to your words, use fresh, original language. Doing so will suggest that you also have fresh, original ideas.

3.5 Excessive Use of Linking Verbs

In business writing, you should strive for vigorous, energetic language. After all, business is about action! Dynamism! Leadership! One of the best ways to increase the vigor of your writing is to avoid the excessive use of **linking verbs**, which are verbs that describe a state of being. The most common linking verb is *to be*, whose basic forms are as follows: *am, is, are, was, were, be, been,* and *being.*

Other examples of linking verbs include *appear, feel, look, seem, sound,* and *smell.* Depending on how they are used, most of these additional examples can sometimes also be **action verbs**, which, as the name indicates, describe action.

For instance, in the following sentence, *appeared* is a linking verb because it describes a state of being.

The manager appeared tired.

But in this next sentence, *appeared* is an action verb because it describes an occurrence; something happens in the sentence.

> The manager appeared in the doorway.

Other examples of action verbs include *repair, arrive, audit, testify, rotate,* and *brainstorm.* These, as well as most other action verbs, can't double as linking verbs.

When you write, you will naturally need to use both linking and action verbs; both verb types play a critical role in the English language. However, the overuse of linking verbs can sometimes leave a piece of writing flat. Where possible, don't just tell what something *is*; tell what it *does*.

Consider the following sentence:

> Mark is tall.

In this example, the linking verb *is* describes a state of being. In the example below, however, a similar concept is expressed with an action verb, *towers*.

> Mark towers over his colleagues.

The two sentences illustrate how the use of an action verb can enliven a sentence. The point is not that the sentence *Mark is tall* is deficient; in fact, depending on the context, it could work perfectly well. However, the choice between *is* and a more active alternative becomes important when linking verbs appear in abundance in a piece of writing.

Compare these two versions of a paragraph from a business letter (key verbs appear in bold-face):

Version 1

There **are** three factors influencing my decision to end partnership discussions with you. First, you **are** not knowledgeable about industry regulations. Second, you **are** often several days late in returning my phone calls. Third—and most important—you **are** not willing to sign an agreement limiting my liability in case the business **is** not successful.

Version 2

Three factors **influenced** my decision to end partnership discussions with you. First, you do not **know** the industry regulations. Second, you often **take** several days to return my phone calls. Third—and most important—you **have refused** to sign an agreement limiting my liability in case the business **fails**.

In the second version, action verbs replaced each instance of *is* or *are* from the first. The second version is crisper and more dynamic.

The next time you write something, circle every linking verb you can find in the document. If you see many of them, you may want to rewrite some of the sentences and substitute some action verbs. Replacing just a few linking verbs with their more active counterparts can transform a page of writing.

One caveat: in seeking out linking verbs, disregard sentences such as the following.

Jen **is rewriting** the letter.

Rob and Pat **are editing** the report.

In both cases, the main verbs are the action verbs — *rewriting* and *editing,* respectively — and the forms of *to be* simply act as **helping verbs**. Here they help by showing, in combination with the *ing* endings on the main verbs, that Jen is in the midst of rewriting, while Rob and Pat are in the midst of editing. (An industrious bunch!) These sentences do not contain linking verbs and are therefore not relevant for this discussion.

Chapter 4

E-Mail: Communication in an Electronic Age

THE ADVENT OF ELECTRONIC MAIL has expedited business communications, but at a cost to clarity and basic business etiquette. Many electronic messages reach their destinations in a state of linguistic chaos, lacking the traditional hallmarks of good business correspondence: a clear purpose, logical organization, and appropriate punctuation and mechanics.

Despite the conversational feel of much computer-based communication, e-mail is a written form and should therefore observe many of the conventions associated with traditional business letters and memos. Work-related e-mail messages should generally include appropriate salutations and closings, signature files, and standard punctuation and capitalization. In addition, in using e-mail's copying and forwarding capabilities, businesspeople should ensure that they are making wise choices and not adding unnecessarily to e-mail volume.

Finally, e-mail should not be viewed as an all-purpose replacement for face-to-face communications. Live interactions, whether on the phone or in person, are valuable tools for building and sustaining professional relationships. Especially in volatile or emotionally fraught situations, e-mail is not a communications cure-all.

4.1 **Anatomy of an E-Mail Message**

In the mid-1990s, if a manager had wanted a document from an employee, he or she might have phoned. The conversation would perhaps have sounded something like this:

Employee: Hello?

Manager: Hi, John. How are you?

Employee: Fine, Janet. How are you?

Manager: Great. I was wondering whether you had a copy of the latest user guide.

Employee: Absolutely. Would you like me to bring it over?

Manager: Yeah, that would be great. Thank you.

Employee: Sure. See you in a minute.

The words themselves would certainly have conveyed information, but our hypothetical employee, John, would also have gleaned additional information from the manager's tone of voice. He would have been able to make reasonable guesses about whether she was in a good mood, pleased with his work, in a hurry, and so on.

Such an exchange might alternatively have taken place in person, in which case John would also have received visual cues through Janet's facial expressions and body language.

Today such an interaction is increasingly likely to take place through e-mail. When a person sends an e-mail, though, vocal and physical cues are absent. Without accompanying nonverbal signals, messages can easily come across as rude, or curt, or confusing—despite the good intentions of the sender.

Salutation

From Samuel Allison <samuel.allison@xyz-inc.com>

To Karen Jones <karen.jones@lmno-inc.com>

Subject Marks report

Dear Karen:

Message Content

Have you completed a revision of the Marks report, and if so, may I have a copy of it? I would like to take it to my meeting with Rachel tomorrow.

I will be in my office until noon if you have any questions.

Closing

Regards,
Sam

Signature File

--
Samuel Allison
Director, Marketing
XYZ, Inc.
123 Anywhere Street
New York, NY 10024
Tel: (212) 555-1234
Fax: (212) 555-3456
samuel.allison@xyz-inc.com
www.xyz-inc.com

Figure 1 • ANATOMY OF AN E-MAIL

Good writing in the context of e-mail messages, many of which are very short, requires an understanding of their various components. Figure 1 on the previous page illustrates these components, some of which are discussed in detail below.

4.1.1 Salutations

The salutation is the opening line of your e-mail where you address the recipient directly, usually by name. In business letters, your choices for salutations are limited to options such as:

Dear Ms. Smith:
Dear Manuel:
To Whom It May Concern:

In the world of e-mail, however, a number of salutation styles are acceptable. Which one is best for a given situation depends on factors such as your relationship to the recipient, the culture of your firm or department, and the content and context of the message. In addition, salutations for a single recipient generally differ from those for multiple recipients.

Listed below are various salutations commonly found in e-mail messages directed to a single recipient. Their inclusion here does not necessarily mean they are broadly acceptable; there are comments elaborating on the relevance and appropriateness of each greeting for business e-mail. The salutations are loosely organized from more formal to less formal.

E-MAIL SALUTATIONS FOR A SINGLE RECIPIENT

Salutation	Comments
To Whom It May Concern:	Although this formulation sounds rather old-fashioned and stuffy, it has long had a place in business letters to unknown recipients. A very formal greeting, it could be appropriate in cases such as an e-mailed inquiry regarding a potential vendor's services or an e-mailed complaint.
Dear Sir or Madam:	This option is similar to the one above.
Dear Mr. Smith:	This formal salutation is appropriate when you are e-mailing a person you do not know well or at all—for example, a prospective client. Depending on your corporate culture, you may also want to use it when writing to someone in your firm who is quite senior to you, particularly if you don't know the person.
Dear James:	Some people find *Dear* along with a first name to be a strange opening for an e-mail, complaining that it feels either too intimate—like a personal letter—or too formal. If you aren't comfortable using *Dear* with co-workers, there are certainly other options, but the salutation *Dear* has a long and happy history in business correspondence. Even if [*Continued*]

E-MAIL SALUTATIONS FOR A SINGLE RECIPIENT, *Cont'd*

	you do not use it much internally at your firm, it has a legitimate place in your e-mail repertoire, particularly for external, international, and formal communications.
James, *James -*	Fine in many contexts. Occasionally the name by itself can sound a little abrupt, but it is a solid opening for many types of e-mail messages.
Good morning, James.	This salutation can be a useful way to begin e-mail messages as it is both businesslike and friendly. Of course, at the time you send the message, it should actually *be* morning in the recipient's time zone.
Hello, James. *Hello, James -*	These salutations may be acceptable for use in a business context with someone you know reasonably well. The punctuation in the second instance is untraditional outside the world of e-mail, but is clear and practical for electronic use.
Hello James,	This salutation is common but is punctuated untraditionally and is therefore not an ideal way to begin an e-mail. (According to standard punctuation rules, the greeting requires a comma between *Hello* and *James*, but then the writer would end up with two commas in a two-word salutation, which looks odd.)

Hi, James.	For use in a business context, these saluta-
	tions are usually too casual. *Hi* is a word better
Hi, James -	reserved for correspondence with friends.
	However, depending on your corporate culture,
	these salutations may be acceptable for com-
	munications with co-workers you know well.
Hi James,	This salutation is very casual and is also punctuated untraditionally. A comma is needed between *Hi* and *James*, but then the salutation will contain two commas in a row, which looks odd. Although this salutation is common, in business e-mail it may be perceived as unprofessional.

As you can see, it isn't easy to figure out how to address an individual. Addressing a group of people through e-mail can pose an even more formidable challenge. To formulate a salutation for multiple people, consider the composition of the group you will be addressing. If you are writing to your co-workers in the marketing department, for example, you could perhaps begin your message with one of the following salutations:

Dear Colleagues:

Dear Marketing Colleagues:

The appropriateness of these salutations, how-ever, depends on the context and your corporate cul-ture. Below are comments on various salutations, some good and some not so good, that appear in group e-mail messages.

E-MAIL SALUTATIONS FOR MULTIPLE RECIPIENTS

Salutation	Comments
Greetings. *Good morning.* *Good afternoon.*	Any of these salutations can be used in e-mail going to multiple recipients. In addition, *Greetings* can act as a salutation in an automatic reply you might set up when you are going to be out of the office.
Dear Sirs: *Dear Gentlemen:*	In a working world populated by both women and men, these salutations are out of date in almost all cases. Theoretically they could still be used with relative safety in a context where every recipient was male, but even in those cases, the formulations would be likely to come across as old-fashioned.
Dear Colleagues:	This salutation is both respectful and friendly. It can be used to address the people in your department or division, assuming that you have a good working relationship with them and that the members of the group are of similar professional status or junior to you. Do not, however, use this salutation with a group containing people senior to you.
Jane and Tim, *Dear Jane and Tim:* *Good morning, Jane and Tim.*	If you are addressing two people, you may use their names in combination with various greetings from the table of e-mail salutations for individual recipients. Some common options appear to the left. For e-mails going to more than two people, it can sound awkward to refer to all of them by name.

[*None*]	Many people don't like to receive e-mails without salutations. Nonetheless, if your corporate culture supports it, sending a mass e-mail with no greeting at all can make sense. Such an e-mail is, after all, virtually identical in form to the traditional memo, which does not contain a greeting.
Hello,	If you can't figure out a way to address your recipients directly, whether as *Marketing Staff*, *Colleagues*, or something else, the first three salutations in this table (*Greetings*, *Good morning*, or *Good afternoon*) may be preferable to the more casual, less professional-sounding *Hello*.
Hi, all! *Hi, all.* *Hi!*	Unless you have a very casual working environment — and even if you do — these formulations can sometimes be perceived as unprofessional. Proceed with caution.
Guys,	Like *Dear Sirs* and *Dear Gentlemen*, this salutation may offend female recipients. In addition, it is too casual for most workplace correspondence.

4.1.2 *Closings*

There are multiple ways to close an e-mail. The first step is to choose your closing word or phrase, if you wish to include one — for example, *Thank you*, or *Sincerely*, or *Regards*. If you know your recipient and are addressing him or her by first name, in most cases you should follow your *Thank you* or *Regards* with your first name. If you are writing more formally and are addressing the recipient by last name, it is usually preferable to use your full name.

Below are some common e-mail closings accompanied by comments on their use.

E-MAIL CLOSINGS

Closing Phrase	Comments
Sincerely,	This is a polite, professional way to close, but is most appropriate for formal e-mails, such as initial communications with prospective clients. In e-mails with people you already know, *Sincerely* may come across as excessively formal.
Regards,	This is a safe, acceptable closing term in almost all situations, ranging from fairly casual to quite formal.
Thank you,	This closing is ideal when you want to show appreciation for something the recipient has done or is going to do for you. (If you want to be very appreciative and say *Thank you very much*, then you can keep that as a separate sentence and perhaps add a different closing. For instance: Thank you very much. Regards, Rose
Thanks,	Similar to *Thank you* above, but more casual. Most appropriate if you are writing [*Continued*]

	to co-workers you know well and have a good relationship with, or when you are e-mailing, say, vendors or people who are somewhat junior to you. If you have reason to be really appreciative, *Thank you* is generally a better choice.
[*None*]	For quick, casual e-mails to people with whom you have an established business relationship, closing with just your first name is a common and acceptable practice.
Best,	Ending with *Best* may give the impression that the e-mail writer was simply too busy to bother completing the closing. Best *what*, after all? It could perhaps be considered the e-mail equivalent of a host's failing to see a guest all the way to the door at the end of a dinner party.

4.1.3 *Signature Files*

A signature file is a block of contact information appearing at the bottom of an e-mail. For example:

Marcia Jackson
Director, Training
XYZ, Inc.
111 Main Street
Anytown, NY 10909
Tel: (212) 555-0469
Fax: (212) 555-1472
marcia.jackson@xyz-inc.com
www.xyz-inc.com

In your e-mail software, there should be an option enabling you to set up a signature file that will then appear automatically in all of your outgoing messages.

Why is a signature file necessary? For one thing, it helps an e-mail appear polished and professional; it is like stationery for electronic messages. In addition, if recipients of a message don't know you very well or at all, the absence of a signature file can cause confusion as they try to figure out who you are. Finally, you should generally make it as easy as possible for recipients to find you; by including contact information in your standard communications, you enable them to reach you with minimal effort.

Your e-mail software may well allow you to set up a shorter, alternative signature file for internal communications with employees of your firm. Suppose, for example, that Marcia Jackson from the previous signature file is e-mailing someone in her company's accounting department. An appropriate signature file for internal use could be:

Marcia Jackson
Director, Training
Tel: (212) 555-0469
Fax: (212) 555-1472

Of course, not every e-mail should have a signature file. Sometimes you may not want people to have your contact information. For example, if you are sending a message asking someone to stop sending you unsolicited e-mail, delete the contact information from your signature file so that you won't give the person even more information than he or she already has!

In addition, if you are having an ongoing e-mail dialogue with someone, it is often better—after your initial exchange—to omit the signature file in subsequent messages that accumulate within the same e-mail chain. That way your contact information won't show up repeatedly within the growing pile of messages.

4.2 **Special Topics**

E-mail offers powerful communication features—and some attendant risks. This section addresses a sampling of communication issues unique to electronic correspondence.

4.2.1 *Copying*

Senders of e-mail can easily copy someone on an outgoing e-mail message. Copying features offer convenience, but they are sometimes used in ways that test the limits of business etiquette. Naturally, you should copy managers who have requested that you copy them on certain types of communications. In addition, if your industry has regulatory requirements regarding the use of e-mail, you should certainly do whatever is necessary to comply with those requirements.

Otherwise, you should generally copy only those people who truly need the information you are sending in a given e-mail. Don't automatically emulate what your co-workers happen to be doing. For example, don't copy five of your colleagues just because you noticed that another of your co-workers did that on his last communication. Perhaps that person's judgment was flawed! The important question is whether those five colleagues really need the information you are sending.

Unfortunately, excessive copying has much to do with the e-mail inundation of American business today. Sending co-workers unnecessary e-mails is irritating to them and counterproductive for your firm.

4.2.2 *Reply All*

One way to reduce e-mail volume is to use the "Reply All" option sparingly. If someone sends a mass e-mail and you want to send a response, in many cases you should choose the "Reply" option, which sends a message just to the sender—and not to all the other original recipients. Of course, if everyone needs to see your response, then "Reply All" is the only choice—but do not choose "Reply All" to send an e-mail consisting of nothing more than "Thanks!" or "Got it."

If you want only a subset of the original recipients to receive your response, select "Reply All" but then, before you send the e-mail, remove names of recipients you don't wish to include. Your response will then go just to an appropriate subset of the original group. A moment of careful thought on your end can save time for many other people.

4.2.3 *Forwarding*

The fact that e-mail can be forwarded so easily creates business communication challenges that did not exist in the past. Although the ability to forward e-mail messages is a powerful feature that allows information to be shared quickly with others, one of the most disturbing habits in modern business correspondence is the unexamined forwarding of messages that were intended for the recipient's eyes only. Before you click "Forward," consider carefully how the sender of the e-mail would feel about having the message passed on to another reader.

Whether it is acceptable to forward a given message depends on various factors, including the relationship between the writer and recipient, their relative status, and the content and context of the message. But in general, forwarding something private or sensitive is likely to reflect poorly not only on the writer, but also on the person who forwards the e-mail.

At the same time, you should write your messages as though they may be forwarded. Forwarded messages have cost careless e-mail writers their jobs, so it is wise to be cautious about what you put in writing. Clearly you shouldn't e-mail inflammatory content.

In addition, it is a good idea to structure e-mail messages so that they can easily be forwarded for maximum benefit. Consider splitting up unrelated topics into multiple e-mails. For instance, in the sample message in Figure 2, the writer of the e-mail combines a message about a marketing report with an apology for arriving late to a morning meeting.

The first part of the e-mail discusses a revision of the report, a subject of potential interest to other employees at the company. Therefore, the message may well be forwarded.

Unfortunately, though, if this e-mail is forwarded in its current form, the allusion to the writer's tardiness will automatically be passed on as well. Instead of providing a purely positive reflection of his efforts on behalf of the company — exemplified by his work on the report — the e-mail will also inform people who would never have known it otherwise that he was tardy to a meeting that morning. In addition, the e-mail contains personal information about family that the writer may not wish to share with others at his firm.

From	George Chen <george.chen@xyz-inc.com>
To	Karen James <karen.james@xyx-inc.com>
Subject	Revision of Online Marketing Report

Karen,

I have attached the latest revision of the online marketing report for your review. I made some substantial changes, including the following:

- deleted several paragraphs in Section 4 that repeated content in Section 2
- added an executive summary
- added various subheadings to help clarify organization

I look forward to hearing your response.

By the way, I'm very sorry I didn't arrive on time for the meeting this morning. My daughter has bronchitis, and I had to take her to the pediatrician on my way to work.

Regards,
George

--
George Chen
Marketing Department
Red Bank Facility
Tel: 918-555-4598
Fax: 918-555-8763

Figure 2 • MESSAGE THAT CAN'T EASILY BE FORWARDED

The writer would be better off doing one of two things: (1) splitting the e-mail into two messages, one apologizing for the tardiness and one addressing the report, or (2) apologizing in person or over the phone for the tardiness and sending an e-mail about the report. In either case, the content relating to the report could then be forwarded to people who may be impressed by it. They will not hear about bronchitis, tardiness, or other personal matters.

4.3 The Limitations of E-Mail

Don't overestimate the utility of e-mail. In this electronic age, people sometimes fail to recognize the value of spoken communication. Preferring e-mail, they avoid face-to-face or phone conversations. This strategy is unwise, because spoken communications are a valuable way to develop and cement professional relationships that can help you throughout your career.

Also, be sensible about the types of subjects you try to address through e-mail. For communications about really important issues — an imminent major deadline, for example — don't assume an e-mail will be enough. In such cases, try phoning instead of or in addition to e-mailing. You can't always be certain that people will see and respond to e-mail quickly, especially if they travel a lot or receive dozens of e-mail messages a day.

Finally, if you sense that an e-mail dialogue is becoming confrontational, stop communicating about the topic online and have a phone conversation — or, even better — a face-to-face discussion with the person. It is much harder to communicate effectively about sensitive topics through the medium of the computer than it is in person or over the phone. By talking things through, you are more likely to keep a situation from spiraling out of control.

Chapter 5

Editing Your Writing: Tips and Tricks

You can spend many hours creating a memo or proposal, but if the first thing readers encounter when they pick up your document is an embarrassing typographical error, some of the good work you've done will instantly be undone. Alternatively, if your ideas are wonderful but the document is wordy and repetitive, your readers may not even heed what you are trying to say.

The good news: careful editing can turn a weak document into a powerful piece of writing. Editing takes place on many levels. It can range from a quick review of a short e-mail message to an exhaustive, and possibly exhausting, revision process involving many document drafts with contributions from multiple writers. This chapter describes tips and tricks used by professional writers and editors, as well as a series of checklists to remind you what to look for as you review your writing. With a systematic approach to editing, you can enhance your ability to address organizational flaws, improve sentence structure and word choice, and find and fix mistakes.

The discussion on the following pages focuses on how to edit your own writing, but most of the concepts apply whether you are revising your document or someone else's. Keep in mind that effective editing sometimes requires ruthlessness. One cannot afford to be timid or indifferent about making changes when important communications are at stake!

1. **Invest in a reference library.** Consider purchasing one or more of the following:

- *a good dictionary*

A small paperback dictionary is helpful, but not sufficient. Smaller dictionaries have the advantage of being more portable, but they also contain less content, so words you need may not be included. If you purchase a print dictionary, buy one with some heft! If you use an online dictionary, make sure the content comes from a reliable source. Your dictionary should also be fairly current, as language is constantly evolving: over time new words are born, old ones can mutate, and other words die.

- *a grammar book*

Syntaxis Press offers *A Grammar Guide for Business Professionals*; for information about the book, please visit www.syntaxis.com. Alternatively, go to a local bookstore and browse the reference section for books whose layout and content you feel comfortable with. Look up a few grammatical issues in the ones that appeal to you most and read the explanations provided in order to determine which book(s) will be most helpful to you.

- *a style guide*

A style guide typically offers advice on an array of writing, usage, and grammar points, but may also provide guidance on layout, format, and various other issues affecting the content and appearance of a piece of writing. There are a number of excellent style guides available. One respected reference work is *The Chicago Manual of Style*, which is available in print or through an online subscription at www.chicagomanualofstyle.org.

2. Use your reference books. It is unfortunately rather common for people to buy dictionaries and other language guides and then leave them unopened on the shelf. Reference books aren't helpful unless their owners refer to them! The more you use them, the more you will learn and the more adept you will become at finding the information you need.

3. Use the editing checklists at the end of this chapter. The checklists cover writing issues ranging from organization to style and word choice, and can remind you of what to look for as you revise.

4. Double-space during the revision process.

In the earlier stages of revising, double-spacing your draft can make it easier to read and edit. Use a font that you find easy to read, even if the final font choice will be different. Some people like to increase the margins temporarily, too, as that makes the text appear less dense. Once you have the content in good shape, you can change the font and layout back to the preferred format.

5. **Print your document.** It is often easier to find typographical errors and other writing problems on a printed page than on the computer screen. Although it can sometimes be more efficient to edit electronically, many writers benefit from a combination of electronic and hard-copy editing.

6. **Outline what you have written.** Many people have been told to create outlines before they begin writing. Fewer people are familiar with outlining as an editing technique that can help them *after* they have finished a draft. In fact, though, outlining is a valuable tool to ensure that a writer is presenting his or her ideas in the best possible order. To create an informal post-draft outline, underline the thesis or main idea of your document. (If you can't find a thesis, rewrite until you have one.) Then read through the entire document, jotting in the margin each new topic you come across. Once you have finished, analyze your thesis and margin notes to see whether you can find any structural failings.

7. Finish your first draft as far ahead of time as you can. If you spread the revision process out over a longer period of time, you will have more opportunities to come to your document fresh and to edit with a clear head.

8. Remember: there is no such thing as too many drafts. Professional writers often go through many, many drafts of a document before they feel satisfied with it. The goal is not to get a piece of writing perfect the first or second time (though if you can, you deserve congratulations!). Rather, the goal is to improve it through careful, thoughtful editing. Obviously you won't have time to write multiple drafts of every e-mail, but the point is, you shouldn't burden yourself with the goal of instant perfection.

9. Remember also: no pain, no gain. Effective editing involves careful thought and hard work; it isn't supposed to be easy. If you find you are suffering mightily through the revision process, keep in mind that people all over the world are experiencing similar or identical feelings this very minute. You are not alone!

10. Don't try to fix everything at once. Generally it is most efficient to edit first for organizational issues and then later for details such as sentence structure, word choice, and grammar. (Otherwise you may be fixing verb forms and comma placement in sentences that you will ultimately cut for structural reasons!) Be flexible, though. If you are perplexed about how to fix an organizational problem, for example, try spending a little time editing for something else: tone, wording, passive voice, and so on. Editing for other issues when you are stuck can be a helpful way to get to know your document better and understand its strengths and weaknesses more thoroughly. Sometimes that greater familiarity will lead to an organizational breakthrough.

11. Ask someone else to look at your document. A fresh perspective can be extremely helpful. If you do a lot of editing, perhaps you and a colleague could even arrange to review each other's documents on an ongoing basis.

12. Review your document word for word. When editing for details such as grammar and word choice, read carefully. That means examining each word to make sure that it is correct and that it expresses accurately what you want to say. If you are editing on a printed page, use your pen or pencil to point at each word individually as you read; doing so can help ensure that you don't skip anything. If you skim your document, it is practically guaranteed that you will miss problem areas.

13. Take advantage of technological tools. The grammar- and spell-checking features of your word-processing software can help you find mistakes. Do not, however, automatically accept every recommendation the software makes. Sometimes it will suggest the wrong word for a given situation, or complain that there is a grammatical error when there is none. Knowledgeable grammarians frequently turn off the grammar-checker, as they are able to find grammatical problems themselves and prefer not to have to wade through all the false error alerts, but the spell-checker is a useful tool for just about everyone.

14. Pay particular attention to your own writing weaknesses. If you know you have a persistent problem with introductions, spend extra time editing your openings. If you make frequent errors with, say, apostrophes, use the text search function in your software to locate any apostrophes quickly and make sure you have used them correctly.

15. Read your document aloud. Reading aloud enables you to hear the rhythm of your writing and thus identify places where the prose is awkward or choppy. It also forces you to read more carefully, making you more likely to notice typographical errors or missing words.

16. Take a break. If you are confronting a particularly tricky editing problem, leave the document alone for a while. Eat an apple (or a cheeseburger if you think that will be more helpful!), return some phone calls, go for a lunchtime jog. With a little distance between you and your editing problem, you will be more likely to find a solution once you return to your document.

Editing Checklists

THE INTRODUCTION

☐ Does your introduction contain a clear thesis (main idea)?

☐ Does the introduction accurately indicate what will be covered in the following pages?

☐ Is your introduction too broad?

☐ Is your introduction too narrow or detailed?

☐ Is your introduction an appropriate length?

☐ Is your introduction likely to engage the reader?

DOCUMENT STRUCTURE

☐ Does every body paragraph help support the document's thesis?

☐ Are the ideas presented in the best possible order?

☐ Are there any complex ideas that should be broken down further into their constituent points?

☐ Is there unnecessary repetition of ideas?

☐ Are there too many very long or very short paragraphs in a row?

☐ Does the document have a conclusion that summarizes key points — without merely repeating the introduction?

Body Paragraphs

☐ Can you determine the main idea of each body paragraph?

☐ Does all of the content in a given body paragraph relate back to that paragraph's main idea?

☐ Do your body paragraphs include appropriate supporting details and examples?

☐ Do any body paragraphs seem too long or too short?

Sentence Structure

☐ Do you see any overly long, convoluted sentences that could be broken down into two or more shorter sentences?

☐ Are there any places in the document where you see too many short, simple sentences in a row?

☐ Do you overuse a particular sentence structure?

☐ Are there any opportunities to replace passive voice with active voice?

☐ Do you use too many consecutive prepositional phrases?

WORD CHOICE

☐ Is your language as precise and clear as it could be?

☐ Do you see any examples of wordiness or unnecessarily ornate phrases that you could replace with more streamlined language?

☐ Does your document contain any clichés or problematic jargon?

☐ Are there any opportunities to replace linking verbs with action verbs?

☐ Did you look up any words you are uncertain about to make sure you are using them correctly?

Conclusion

NEARLY EVERY WRITER confronts moments of black despair when it seems there is absolutely no solution to a particular writing problem. If that happens to you, take a break. Work on something else for a while to give your head a chance to clear. Often having a little distance from a writing problem will help you come up with a solution.

If you don't have the luxury of a break, press on. Don't panic—just keep crossing out words, rearranging ideas, adding new content, and so on, and eventually something will hit you. The key is to keep trying. Remember: what separates good writers from weaker writers is often little more than hard work.

Index

acronyms, 52–53
action verbs, 54–57, 88
active voice, 38–40, 88
adverbs, conjunctive, 30–32
audience (reader)
    awareness, 2, 10, 13, 15,
        17, 19, 30, 38, 48, 50,
        52–53, 79
    engaging the, 10, 23–24,
        54, 86

to be
    forms of, 36, 37, 54, 57
    overuse of, 54–57, 88
    in passive voice, 36, 37
because, beginning a sen-
    tence with, 32–35
biographies, executive, 14–15
body, of a document, 10,
    11–18, 19, 86, 87
body paragraphs, 15–18, 86,
    87
brainstorming, 8, 9
business correspondence,
    48–50, 59, 63, 67, 73.

    See also business letters;
    e-mail; memos
business letters, 1, 10, 19,
    48–49, 56, 59, 62, 63
business plans, 2

capitalization, 59
choppiness, 18, 23–24, 27, 85
chronological order, 13–15
clarity, 1, 2, 10, 11, 13, 23, 45,
    46, 51, 59, 86, 88
clauses, 24–27
    dependent (subordinate),
        25–26, 32–35
    independent, 25–32, 34, 35
clichés, 53–54, 88
comma splices, 28
commas, 27, 28, 30, 31, 64,
    65, 83–84
conciseness, 2, 11, 38–39, 42,
    48–50, 88
conclusions, 10, 12, 18–19, 87
conjunctions
    coordinating, 29–30
    subordinating, 25–26,

32–35
conjunctive adverbs, 30–32
coordinating conjunctions,
    29–30

dependent clauses, 25–26,
    32–35
details, 8, 12, 13, 15–17, 19, 30,
    46–47, 86, 87
development, 13, 15–17
dictionaries, 47, 80, 81, 88
drafts, 7, 9, 11, 19–20, 47, 79,
    82, 83

editing. 1, 20, 47, 79–88. *See
    also* rewriting
e-mail, 1, 6, 48–49, 59–77,
    79, 83
    closings, 59, 61, 67–69
    copying, 59, 71–72
    dialogues, 71, 77
    format, 60–71
    forwarding, 59, 73–76
    limitations of, 59–60,
        76–77
    "Reply All" function,
        72–73
    salutations, 59, 61, 62–67
    signature files, 59, 61,
        69–71
examples, 12, 13–14, 15, 19, 87
executive biographies, 14–15

fragments, sentence, 8,

34–35
freewriting, 8–9

grammar, 8, 9, 24, 34–35,
    36, 80–81, 83, 84, 85
grammar-checker, 6, 84–85

helping verbs, 57

independent clauses, 25–32,
    34, 35
introductions, 9–12, 18–19,
    85, 86, 87

jargon, 2, 50–53, 88

letters. *See* business letters
linking verbs, overuse of,
    54–57, 88
logical order, 13; 14

main idea
    of a body paragraph,
        15–18, 87
    of a document, 10, 12,
        18–19, 20, 82, 86
marketing writing, 1, 46–47
memos, 1, 9, 12, 19, 48–49,
    51–52, 59, 67, 79
most important idea first,
    12–13, 14–15

natural language, 1, 48–50
nouns, 24, 41

proper, 25

order of ideas, 12–15, 82, 86
organization, 1, 5–20, 59,
    74–76, 79, 81, 82, 83–84,
    86–87
ornate language, 48–50, 88
outlines, 9, 82

paragraphs, 5–6, 20
    body, 15–18, 86, 87
    concluding, 10, 12, 18–19,
        87
    introductory, 9–12, 18–19,
        85, 86, 87
    length of, 6, 10–11, 17–18,
        87
passive voice, 35–40, 84, 88
past participles, 36–38
periods, 27
    vs. commas, 28
    vs. semicolons, 27
precision, 45–47, 88
predicate, 24–26
prepositional phrases, 37
    excessive use of, 41–42, 88
prewriting, 7–9
pronouns, 24, 41
proper nouns, 25
proposals, 1, 10, 79
punctuation
    between clauses, 26–35
    commas, 27, 28, 30, 31,
        64, 65, 83–84

in e-mail, 59, 64, 65
    periods, 27, 28
    semicolons, 27–29, 31

reader. *See* audience
repetitive writing, 20, 79, 87
reports, 1, 9, 10–11, 13, 17, 18,
    19
research, 2, 7–8, 9
revising. *See* rewriting.
rewriting (revising), 3, 6, 7,
    10, 11–12, 16, 19–20, 38,
    39, 42, 45, 47, 48, 49–50,
    56–57, 79–88. *See also*
    editing
run-on sentences, 26–27

salutations, e-mail, 59, 61,
    62–67
semicolons, 27–29, 31
    vs. periods, 27
sentence fragments, 8,
    34–35
sentences
    length of, 23–24, 87
    punctuation of, 27–32
    run-on sentences, 26–27
    structure of, 10, 23–42,
        79, 83, 87–88
    variety, 23, 26–35, 88
signature files, 59, 61, 69–71
spell-checker, 6, 84–85
spelling, 9, 84–85
structure. *See* organization

style, writing, 1, 26–27, 28, 30, 31–32, 33, 49, 62, 81
subject
    grammatical, 24–26, 33, 36, 38
    knowing your, 2, 7–8
subordinate clauses, 25. *See also* dependent clauses
subordinating conjunctions, 25–26, 32–35

thesis, 10, 12, 82, 86. *See also* main idea, of a document
tone, 60–61, 84
topic sentences, 17. *See also* main idea, of a body paragraph
training materials, 13
transitional expressions, 6–7
typographical errors, 79, 82, 85

user guides, 13

verbosity. *See* wordiness
verbs, 24, 33, 36–37, 83–84
    action, 54–57, 88
    to be, forms of, 36, 37, 54, 57
    helping, 57
    linking, 54–57, 88
    past participles, 36–38

word choice, 6, 7, 10, 45–57, 79, 81, 83–84, 88
wordiness, 33, 38–39, 42, 48–50, 79, 88
writer's block, 8–9
writing process, 2, 6–9, 19–20